297

religion in focus
islam

Geoff Teece

W
FRANKLIN WATTS
LONDON•SYDNEY

First published in Great Britain by
Franklin Watts
96 Leonard Street
LONDON EC2A 4XD

Franklin Watts Australia
45–51 Huntley Street
Alexandria
NSW 2015

ISBN: 0 7496 4796 5

A CIP catalogue record for this book is available from the British Library

Printed in Malaysia

Series Editor: Adrian Cole
Editor: Susie Brooks
Designer: Proof Books
Art Director: Jonathan Hair
Consultant: Usamah K. Ward,
Education Officer for
the Muslim Educational Trust
Picture Researcher: Diana Morris

Acknowledgements
The publishers would like to thank
the following for permission to
reproduce photographs in this book:

Bettman/Corbis: 11t.
Christine Osborne/Corbis: 27.
Christine Osborne/World Religions
PL: front cover, back cover, 3, 5, 6, 13,
15, 16, 19, 22, 24, 25, 26t, 26b, 29.
K. Pratt/World Religions PL: 23.
H Rogers/Trip: 7, 8, 18, 30.
Pam Smith/Eye Ubiquitous: 28.
Syder/World Religions PL: 1, 20.
Trip: 2, 10, 11b, 12, 14, 17t, 17b.
Julia Waterlow/Eye Ubiquitous: 21.

Whilst every attempt has been made to clear
copyright should there be any inadvertent
omission please apply to the publisher
regarding rectification.

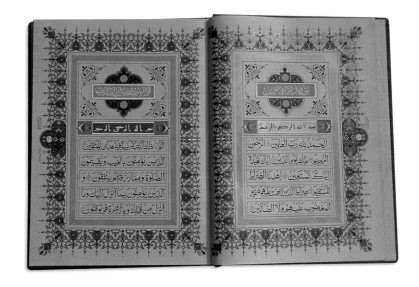

A SIGN OF RESPECT

To show respect for the prophets, Muslims often write or say the Arabic phrase ﷺ (*sallallahu 'alaihi wassalam*), which means 'peace and blessings of Allah be upon him' (pbuh), after the prophets names. In this book we have written 'pbuh' or 'pbut' (peace and blessings of Allah be upon them) as a sign of respect.

Contents

Islam is one of the great world religions. The word 'Islam' means 'submitting to the will of Allah', and anyone who practises this faith is called a Muslim – 'someone who submits to the will of Allah'. Islam originated in Saudi Arabia, but today it is the main religion in more than 60 different countries.

THE MUSLIM POPULATION

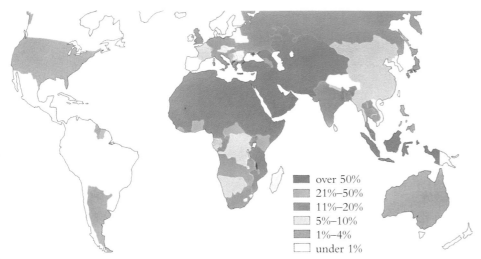

over 50%
21%–50%
11%–20%
5%–10%
1%–4%
under 1%

This map shows the percentage of Muslims in the population of each country. Today, there are an estimated 1.4 billion Muslims in the world. Most Muslims live in Central Asia and North Africa. Almost 10 million live in the USA and over 1.5 million live in the UK.

ALLAH'S MESSAGE

Islam is part of a religious tradition which shares its origins with Christianity and Judaism. But Muslims actually regard their religion as timeless. They believe that there is one God, who in Arabic is called Allah, and that He has revealed one eternal message since the beginning of time. This message was spread to humankind by many prophets, beginning with Adam (pbuh), the first man.

According to Islam, the prophets were all Muslims because they obeyed and submitted to Allah. Muslims believe that over time the prophets' teachings were distorted by other humans. So, to remind people of His original Word, Allah sent further prophets, including Nuh, Ismail and Musa (pbut, see page 9). The last, and most important prophet, was Muhammad (pbuh).

MUHAMMAD (pbuh), THE SEAL OF THE PROPHETS

By the 6th century CE, people had lost sight of the early prophets' guidance and worshipped different kinds of god. The guidance of the Prophet Muhammad (pbuh) brought people back to the religion of the one God. He was born around 570 CE in the city of Makkah, in a country now called Saudi Arabia. Muslims do not believe that Muhammad (pbuh) brought a new faith into the world. He completed the series of prophets who, over time, had brought Allah's original message to the people of the world. That is why he is sometimes called the 'seal of the prophets'.

WRITTEN WORD

Muslims respect the early prophets' scriptures, such as the *Torah* (of Prophet Musa (pbuh)) and the Gospels (of Prophet Isa (pbuh)). But Muslims believe that over time these became distorted versions of Allah's original Word. They believe the final and truest form of Allah's message was revealed to the Prophet Muhammad (pbuh) and is written in their holy book, the Qur'an (see pages 12–13).

MUHAMMAD'S (pbuh) SUCCESSORS

Muhammad (pbuh) died in 632 CE. For 30 years after his death, Muslims were governed in turn by four caliphs (successors). These were Abu Bakr, Umar, Uthman and Ali. Most Muslims call all four successors 'the rightly guided caliphs'. After the death of Uthman, Ali became Caliph. But he was challenged by a rival and eventually killed, as was his son, Husain.

Two groups

The situation resulted in the formation of two groups within the Islamic faith. Those Muslims who followed Ali because he was related to Muhammad (pbuh), and who believed Ali should have been the first caliph, became known as the Shi'ah. Other Muslims became known as Sunnis, a name which comes from the word 'sunnah', meaning 'the practice of the Prophet' (pbuh). The Sunnis make up about 80 per cent of the world's Muslim population, the Shi'ahs about 20 per cent.

MUSLIMS IN MOROCCO
These Sunni Muslims are part of a Muslim population that stretches across the world.

THE SPREAD OF ISLAM

When Muhammad (pbuh) died, over half of Arabia was Muslim. During the next 100 years Islam spread rapidly to places such as Spain in the West and India in the East. By 712 CE Islam had reached China and Tibet. Today, most Muslims live in Central Asia and North Africa. In Afghanistan, 99 per cent of the population is Muslim, in Pakistan 97 per cent, and in Bangladesh 83 per cent.

Muslim beliefs about Allah

THE ONENESS OF ALLAH

Muslims believe strongly in the oneness, or Unity, of Allah. In Islam this is called *tawhid*. *Tawhid* refers to Allah, the Creator and Sustainer of all things. As the Qur'an says: 'No son did Allah beget, nor is there any god along with Him' (*Qur'an 23:91*). Worshipping anything apart from Allah, or comparing anything to Him, is considered a great sin. Allah creates everything in the universe and only Allah is uncreated. Nothing happens in the world that is not willed by Allah. This belief in the Unity of Allah is the focus of the Islamic religion.

THE SHAHADAH

THE SHAHADAH

This *shahadah* is written on the tiled *qiblah* wall of a mosque in Pakistan.

A Muslim's belief in Allah is expressed most simply and clearly in the *shahadah*. This is a statement of faith, which declares: 'I bear witness that there is no god but Allah and I bear witness that Muhammad [pbuh] is His messenger.' It is the first duty of all Muslims to make this declaration of faith and it is often written on the *qiblah* wall of a mosque (see page 20).

ALLAH'S ATTRIBUTES

According to Islam, the essence of Allah is beyond all human understanding. But the relationship between Allah and human beings can be understood by looking at the creation of the first human, Adam (pbuh). The Qur'an tells us that Allah taught Adam (pbuh) the names of all things. This means that human beings were given understanding of the world around them. The essence of every created thing reflects an attribute (characteristic) of Allah, and humans are the only creatures who have been given the ability to recognise these attributes.

The attributes of Allah are perfect and eternal. For human beings, they provide the perfect example of qualities such as mercy, justice, truth, goodness and beauty. These are all qualities that humans have the potential to develop.

FAITH

Muslims refer to the human gift of recognising Allah's attributes as 'faith' or *iman*. Faith enables Muslims to see the beauty of Allah in a flower, for example, or His power in a thunderstorm, or the greatness and infinite nature of Allah in the sky. So humans are thought to have a spiritual side, even though – as earthly creatures – they can be greedy, selfish and cruel. This spirituality is often hidden, but if people submit themselves to Allah and follow the guidance of Muhammad (pbuh), they will realise the God-given qualities they have inside. This will give them heart (*qalb*) and make them peace-loving promoters of Allah.

THE POWER OF ALLAH
Faith, or *iman*, enables Muslims to recognise the power of Allah in scenes such as this sunrise through storm clouds in Morocco.

THE 99 NAMES OF ALLAH

In Islam, Allah has 99 known names. These names refer to the attributes of Allah that Muslims need to remember, study and meditate upon. The Prophet Muhammad (pbuh) is reported as saying: 'There are 99 names that are Allah's alone. Whoever learns, understands and enumerates them enters Paradise and achieves eternal salvation.' Allah is also said to have a 100th name, but this is hidden from humankind because Allah can never be fully understood by any earthly being. Humans can approach Allah but cannot identify themselves with Him.

SOME OF THE 99 NAMES OF ALLAH (TRANSLATED FROM ARABIC):

The Dispenser of Grace, The Merciful;

The Most Gracious, The Beneficent;

The Giver of Faith, The Bestower of Security;

The Source of Peace, Security and Safety;

The Holy;

The Sovereign Supreme;

The Creator;

The Almighty;

The Provider;

The Superior Force;

The Forgiver;

The Maker;

The Honourer;

The All-Knowing;

The Aware;

The Just;

The Judge;

The All-Seeing;

The All-Hearing;

The Protector, The Keeper;

The Great;

The Limitless;

The Infinite; The Answerer;

The Watchful;

The Strong;

The Wise.

Messengers of Allah

GENEALOGY TREE

This illustration shows the direct descendants of Adam (pbuh) through to Muhammad (pbuh). It is important for Muslims to learn about the life and teachings of Muhammad (pbuh). They believe he set a faultless example for human beings.

Muslims believe that a messenger or prophet is someone sent by Allah to spread his message to other people. Prophets were not like normal human beings. Allah gave them the gift of prophethood from birth, so they had qualities which no one else could have or earn, even through prayer or devotion to Allah.

In Arabic, the word for prophet is *nabi*. The plural of *nabi* is *anbiya*. Among the prophets are those who received messages directly from Allah and these prophets are known as *rusul* (messengers). The others were preachers of previous messages. Musa (pbuh), for example, was a prophet and a *rasul*, but his brother Harun (pbuh) was simply a prophet because it was through Musa (pbuh) that Allah revealed new laws.

THE PROPHET MUHAMMAD (pbuh)

It is important for Muslims to study the life of Muhammad (pbuh), and his teachings contained within the *Hadith* (see page 13). He set a faultless example for human beings. However, Muslims do not believe he was divine – but they do believe his message was.

EARLY LIFE

Muhammad (pbuh) was born in Makkah, Saudi Arabia, in 570 CE. His father died before he was born and his mother died when he was only six years old. So, Muhammad (pbuh) was raised by his uncle, Abu Talib.

From childhood, Muhammad (pbuh) worshipped the one God, Allah, and rejected other gods and idols that people around him worshipped. He believed that society in Makkah was often unjust, corrupt, materialistic and cruel. As he grew up, Muhammad (pbuh) worked to help the poor and suffering. He was well liked and came to be seen as wise. He was given the name *al-Amin*, which means 'trustworthy'.

THE 25 PROPHETS

The Qur'an names 25 prophets:

	Islamic name	Biblical name
1	Adam	Adam
2	Idris	Enoch
3	Nuh	Noah
4	Hud	—
5	Salih	—
6	Ibrahim	Abraham
7	Ismail	Ishmael
8	Ishaq	Isaac
9	Lut	Lot
10	Ya'qub	Jacob
11	Yusuf	Joseph
12	Shu'aib	—
13	Ayyub	Job
14	Musa	Moses
15	Harun	Aaron
16	Dhul-Kifl	Ezekiel
17	Dawud	David
18	Sulaiman	Solomon
19	Ilyas	Elias
20	Al Yasa'	Elisha
21	Yunas	Jonah
22	Zakariyyah	Zechariah
23	Yahya	John
24	Isa	Jesus
25	Muhammad	—

(peace and blessings of Allah be upon them all)

THE FIRST REVELATION

When Muhammad (pbuh) was 25 he married Khadijaha, a successful businesswoman whom he had impressed with his ability and character. But, from that time onwards, he began to withdraw himself from everyday life. He often went to a cave in Mount Hira, which lies between Makkah and a place called Mina, and spent days and nights in meditation – especially during the month of *Ramadan* (see page 24).

At the age of 40, Muhammad (pbuh) received his first revelation from the Angel Jibril. The angel said: 'Recite. In the Name of the Lord who created, created Man from a blood clot. Recite. And the Lord is the Most Generous who taught by the Pen, taught Man, that he knew not' (*Qur'an 96:1–5*). This experience had a huge effect on Muhammad (pbuh). He spent the next 13 years spreading the word of the Lord, as the angel had commanded. He preached to the people of Makkah, secretly at first, but openly later on, asking them to reject their different idols and to worship the one God, Allah.

THE PROPHET'S CAVE
The cave in Mount Hira, Saudi Arabia, is now a popular place of pilgrimage for many Muslims.

THE HIJRAH

Most people in Makkah refused to accept Muhammad's (pbuh) message and for two years Muslims were persecuted by the rulers of Makkah. In 622 CE, after the death of his wife Khadijaha, Muhammad (pbuh) was commanded by Allah to go to Madinah. Some of Muhammad's (pbuh) followers had already visited Madinah to preach Islam. There were also some tribal leaders in Madinah who had met Muhammad (pbuh) in Makkah and had become Muslims.

Muhammad's (pbuh) migration is called *hijrah*, and it is from this time that the Islamic calendar is calculated. So 622 CE became year 1 AH (anno Hegirae), and the month of the *hijrah*, called *Muharram*, became the first month of the Muslim year.

IN MADINAH

Muhammad (pbuh) spent 10 years in Madinah. During this time, he received more detailed revelations from Allah, which included details about prayer, fasting, charity, pilgrimage and ways of improving society. In Makkah the revelations had only been short and were mainly linked to beliefs about Allah and the Day of Judgement (see page 29).

BATTLE BETWEEN THE CITIES

Because of religious differences, relations were not good between the cities of Makkah and Madinah. Two significant battles were fought during Muhammad's (pbuh) time. In 624 CE (3 AH), the Battle of Badr saw a small group of Muhammad's (pbuh) Muslim followers defeat a much larger army from Makkah. The following year the Muslims lost the Battle of Uhud against a huge Makkan army. In 627 CE (6 AH) Madinah was under attack from the Makkans but survived due to a trench being dug around it. This led to a peace treaty that allowed Muslims to visit Makkah on pilgrimage.

MAKKAH IS CAPTURED

However, in 630 CE (9 AH), the peace treaty was broken and an army of 20,000 Muslims, led by Muhammad (pbuh), advanced on Makkah. The city was captured without any bloodshed – Muhammad's (pbuh) only aim was to destroy the idols of the city. In 632 CE (11 AH) he went to Makkah on pilgrimage for the last time, and in so doing established *hajj* (see page 17). Before he passed away later that year, Muhammad (pbuh) gave a farewell sermon that included the enforcing of the Five Pillars of Islam (see pages 14–17).

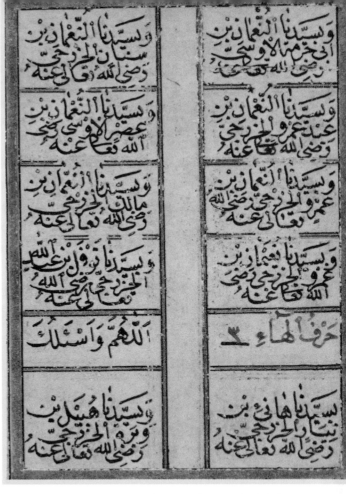

PAGE FROM MARTYRS OF THE BATTLE OF BADR
This page of Arabic text was written in 1836. It documents the events at the Battle of Badr.

PROPHET'S MOSQUE IN MADINAH, SAUDI ARABIA
This mosque is where the Prophet Muhammad (pbuh) is buried.

The Five Pillars

The Five Pillars of Islam are the duties that support the whole way of life for a Muslim. Practising the Five Pillars is a way of obeying Allah and following the practice of Muhammad (pbuh). The Pillars help Muslims to realise their true self and become the kind of human beings that Allah wants them to be. This is only true, of course, if the rituals of the Five Pillars are performed with sincerity and the right intention (*niyyah*).

FIRST PILLAR: THE SHAHADAH

The First Pillar is a statement of belief in one God, called the *shahadah* (see page 6), which underpins everything else that a Muslim does. The *shahadah* recognises that Allah is more important than anything else, and that Muhammad (pbuh) was His final messenger. The *shahadah* is said as often as possible. By reciting the *shahadah*, Muslims express their intention to follow the path and example of the Prophet (pbuh) as closely as possible. A Muslim must be prepared to turn his or her whole life towards Allah.

SECOND PILLAR: SALAH

The Qur'an says: 'Preserve prayer and especially the middle prayer' (*2:238*). Prayer in this sense refers to *salah*, five set prayers that must be said daily – just before sunrise (*fajr*), just after midday (*zuhr*), in the afternoon (*asr*), just after sunset (*maghrib*) and during the night but before midnight (*isha*).

WUDU

Muslims believe that people should put their hearts into prayer – it must not become just a routine exercise. Muhammad (pbuh) taught that if the intention of prayer is wrong, it is unacceptable to Allah. To ensure that the intention is right, a person must prepare properly and perform acts of purification. This is called *wudu*.

Wudu symbolises the cleansing of the body on the inside – a vital theme in Islamic worship. Parts of the body are washed in a set way. The hands are washed three times and the person asks Allah to cleanse them of sins. Next, the nostrils are cleansed three times and the person prays that they may be pure enough to smell the sweetness of Paradise.

The face is then washed three times so that it may display the light of Allah. Both arms are washed, with a prayer to place the person with the

PRAYING
Muslims believe they should put their hearts into prayer. For this reason Muslims perform *wudu*.

righteous, not the sinners, on the Day of Judgement (see page 29). Then the palm of the hand is passed over the head, moving from the top of the forehead to the back. Both hands now pass over the back of the neck, with a prayer that suffering may not 'hang around' the neck. The ears are then rinsed to help the person grow pure in character. Finally, both feet are washed, the right for righteousness and the left in the hope that the person may be saved from sin.

OFFERING SALAH

After *wudu*, a person is ready to offer *salah*. In Islam, the first requirement for any prayer is that the worshipper faces Makkah. Muslims believe that this is where Adam (pbuh) built the first House of Allah, modelled on one in heaven called the *Ka'bah*. The direction of Makkah is always clearly marked in a mosque (see page 20).

Each of the five daily prayers has a fixed set of actions called *rak'ah*. In this way the *rak'ah* shows a person submitting gradually to Allah. After the first *rak'ah* is complete, the person sits back before performing another series of the same actions. The four basic *rak'ahs* are:

WASHING BEFORE PRAYERS
These Muslims in Malaysia are washing before they go to pray in the mosque.

Standing (*qiyam*) – this position varies. In one version the hands are raised to the ears (men) or shoulders (women) before being folded in front of the person.

Bowing (*ruku'*) – with hands placed above the knees.

Prostrating (*sujud*) – with the forehead and nose touching the floor.

Sitting (*julus*) – this position varies. In one version the left leg and foot are folded under the body and the right foot rests on toes that are turned towards the *qiblah* wall.

Each prayer requires a different number of *rak'ahs*:

Fajr	2 rak'ahs
Zuhr	4 rak'ahs
Asr	4 rak'ahs
Maghrib	3 rak'ahs
Isha	4 rak'ahs

As well as performing *rak'ahs*, a Muslim recites set words from memory. These words consist of praise for Allah and quotations from the Qur'an. When the correct number of *rak'ahs* are completed the worshipper turns his or her head to the right and then to the left. These actions are accompanied by a prayer, which grants Allah's blessing and peace to people all around. On Friday there is a special congregational prayer (see page 23).

THIRD PILLAR: ZAKAH

The third Pillar of Islam is *zakah*, which is giving money to the poor. Very often this is paid at the end of *Ramadan* (see page 24). *Zakah* recognises that all good things are a gift from Allah. It also teaches Muslims to support the Muslim community (*ummah*) and people in need in general. *Zakah* is often known as the 'poor due' because all Muslims have a duty to give it and the poor have a right to receive it.

Muslims contribute 2.5 per cent of their savings to *zakah*. Those who have no savings do not have to pay it. In some Islamic countries it operates like a tax and is collected by the government. In non-Muslim areas, Muslims will often send the money to developing countries such as Bangladesh or India. This illustrates the Muslim sense of identity and their duty to the worldwide *ummah*. As well as helping others, *zakah* benefits the giver by removing greed and selfishness. It is a statement of the desire for a fairer society where divisions between rich and poor are broken down.

ZAKAH

Giving money to the poor is the third Pillar of Islam. It teaches Muslims to support the Muslim community (*ummah*).

FOURTH PILLAR: SAWM

Sawm, or fasting, reflects the periods of time when Muhammad (pbuh) went away to meditate (see page 10). It is the duty of all adult Muslims to fast during the daylight hours of the month of *Ramadan* (see page 24) though there are some exceptions. Pregnant women or women having their period, those with illness, those travelling and the elderly are excused. They should make up the lost fast days if they can, but if not, they should help to feed the poor. Children under 12 do not have to fast, but many begin to practise fasting by giving up certain foods for short lengths of time.

Fasting is both external and internal. Those fasting should not eat, drink, or have sexual intercourse between dawn and sunset. The fast is broken each day at sunset with a light meal (*iftar*), beginning with a glass of water and some dates.

There are several reasons for fasting. For Muslims the most important is so that they can gain *Taqwa*, which means 'piety' or 'consciousness of Allah'. Fasting helps Muslims to become more aware of the Creator and the duties He expects from them. It also helps them to identify with those who suffer hunger and thirst in the world. Through fasting, Muslims can learn to control their physical desires, rather than be controlled by them.

FIFTH PILLAR: HAJJ

Hajj is a mass pilgrimage to Makkah that takes place once a year. All Muslims must make the pilgrimage at least once in their lifetime if they are able. However, not everyone manages this, because a pilgrim should be a responsible adult, he or she should be able to afford the trip without leaving the family in debt (*hajj* can cost thousands of pounds) and the person should be physically fit enough to cope.

Hajj itself takes five or six days. It happens in the month of *Dhul-Hijjah*, the 12th month of the Islamic calendar (see page 24). There are various ceremonies that take place over the time of the pilgrimage, and pilgrims visit a number of sacred sites that are important in the history of Islam.

During *hajj*, men must wear *ihram* – two pieces of white cloth. Women can wear whatever is most comfortable – usually a long dress and headcovering – as long as they cover their hair, shoulders and ankles (some women also wear a veil). *Ihram* is a sign of purity and equality. When everyone wears the same simple clothes no distinctions can be made between rich and poor. This teaches all Muslims that everyone is equal in the sight of Allah.

Men who have been on *hajj* are referred to as *hajji* and women as *hajja*. They feel that performing *hajj* is a great privilege and are respected by the rest of the community. *Hajj* strengthens a Muslim's faith and helps them to submit to Allah.

KA'BAH AT HAJJ
Pilgrims pray towards the *Ka'bah* in Makkah during *hajj*. They must also walk round the *Ka'bah*.

HAJJ PILGRIMS
These men are wearing *ihram* – simple clothes that symbolise purity and equality.

BISMILLAH CEREMONY

In some Muslim cultures, when a child reaches the age of four or five, there is a Bismillah ceremony. This introduces the child to reciting passages from the Qur'an and to writing the first letters of the Arabic alphabet. He or she is dressed in new clothes and is made to repeat the opening section of the Qur'an with a religious relative or an *'alim* (learned man). The child is also given a board on which to write his or her first Arabic letters. Gifts of sweets are given in celebration.

MARRIAGE

Muslims believe that Allah wants people to live together as families. This means that marriage is taken very seriously. For Muslims a marriage is not just the joining of two individuals, who must give their consent freely, but the coming together of two families.

Generally, Muslim women are not allowed to marry men who are not Muslims. A Muslim man, however, may marry a woman if she is a practising Christian or Jew and he should not force her to become a Muslim. Sexual relations are forbidden outside wedlock and a woman should not have more than one husband. In special cases, if the law of the country allows, a man may have up to four wives but he must treat them all equally. A man must give a dowry (some property or money) to the woman he is marrying. A woman's main responsibility is to look after and care for the family, although their role varies from country to country.

RECEIVING WEDDING GIFTS
As part of the wedding ceremony, this married couple in Kashmir receive gifts from the rest of the family.

MARRIAGE CEREMONIES

Muslim wedding ceremonies vary greatly, as Islam does not dictate how the event should be celebrated. A Muslim wedding may be held at home or in a mosque. On the day of the marriage, the groom leads his family to the bride's house, or wherever the ceremony is to take place. It is usually the *imam* who conducts the service, and the couple are seated together during the ceremony. The *imam* first asks the woman if she is willing to marry the man. Sometimes this is asked three times. Then the *imam* calls on the man to recite some words from the Qur'an before asking if he will marry the woman. The *imam* finally declares the couple married and, on some occasions, a marriage contract is signed. Traditionally, the couple receive gifts from relatives and friends.

The details of Muslim marriage ceremonies vary worldwide. Many Muslims in Asia include the painting of *mehandi* patterns on the hands and feet of the bride. There are often lavish celebrations after the ceremony, which may depend on the culture of the country in which they are held. In poorer areas, people may borrow money so that they can put on a full-size wedding.

DEATH

Muslims believe in life after death. This centres on the Day of Judgement, when a dead person is asked to account for his or her life on Earth. The person's answer will determine whether they join the sinners or the righteous in the next world. To help a dying person answer correctly, the *shahadah* may be spoken into his or her ear. The person may be placed facing Makkah and, therefore, looking in the direction of the *Ka'bah* (see page 15).

When a person dies, friends and relatives visit the family to comfort them. Prayers are said and people read from the Qur'an. The Prophet Muhammad (pbuh) gave detailed descriptions about what should happen to the dead person. The body should be washed ritually at least three times. This must start at the right side of the body and follow the process of *wudu* (see page 14). The person is being prepared for a last prayer. Perfume is often placed in the hair and on parts of the body used in prayer – the hands, feet, knees and forehead.

After being washed, the body is wrapped in a simple white shroud. Depending on when a person dies, the body may be taken to a mosque for Friday Prayer.

Muslims bury their dead because they believe the person's body will take on a new life. At the graveside, the *imam* says a special prayer and recites these words from the Qur'an: 'We have created you from this earth and We shall return you into it and then shall bring you forth out of it once again' (*Surah 20:55*). The body is then placed on its side in the grave, facing Makkah. Muslim graves are simple. According to Islam, all people are equal in the sight of Allah and so special decorative headstones are not encouraged.

REMEMBERING A LOVED ONE, PAKISTAN
Muslims bury their dead, but are not encouraged to place decorative headstones on the grave as all people are equal in the sight of Allah.

Key questions and answers

WHAT IS ISLAM? Islam originated in Saudi Arabia, but today it is the main religion in more than 60 different countries.

HOW MANY MUSLIMS ARE THERE? 1.4 billion (worldwide estimate). About 80 per cent of the population is Sunni Muslim and about 20 per cent is Shi'ah Muslim (see page 5).

WHAT DO MUSLIMS BELIEVE? Muslims believe that there is one God, called Allah, and that He has revealed one eternal message since the beginning of time. The final and truest form of Allah's message was revealed to the Prophet Muhammad (pbuh, c. 570-632 CE). Muslims believe strongly in the Unity of Allah, called *tawhid*. This is expressed most simply and clearly in the *shahadah* (see pages 6 and 14).

WHAT ARE THE MUSLIM TEACHINGS AND VALUES? Muslims follow the teachings of the prophets (pbut, see pages 8–9). Muhammad (pbuh) taught Muslims that the bond of Islam was stronger than any other ties, and that they were members of the Muslim *ummah* (community). The Five Pillars of Islam are the duties that support the whole way of life for a Muslim (see pages 14–17). Muslims have strict food and drink rules (see page 26).

WHAT ARE THE MUSLIM SCRIPTURES CALLED? The Muslim holy book is called the Qur'an (see pages 12–13). It is the Word of Allah, and was revealed to Muhammad (pbuh). The Qur'an is split into 114 *Surahs*. Muslims also have the *Hadith*. This refers to records of Muhammad's (pbuh) words and deeds.

WHERE DO MUSLIMS WORSHIP? Muslims worship in a mosque (see pages 20–23). They all have a *qiblah* wall in the prayer hall. The *imam* conducts prayers on a Friday. Most mosques provide education in a school called the *madrasah,* and have a separate washing area where worshippers can perform *wudu* (see pages 14–15).

WHAT ARE THE MUSLIM FESTIVALS? Muslim festivals include: *Ashura, Malid al-Nabi, Ramadan, Id-ul-Fitr* and *Id-ul-Adha.*

Glossary

ADHAN Call to prayer.

BISMILLAH-IR-RAHMAN-IR-RAHIM 'In the name of Allah, the merciful, the compassionate.' Begins all *Surahs* of the Qur'an, except the ninth.

DU'A A type of blessing or 'prayer' said by Mulims in hundreds of daily situations, for example before and after eating food. *Du'a* are not accompanied by any actions.

FANA Self-noughting. To get rid of self-centredness.

HADITH A statement or report. The *Hadith* are records of Muhammad's (pbuh) words and deeds during his time as Prophet.

HAFIZ (plural: *huffaz*) The name given to people who memorise the whole of the Qur'an.

HAJJ Annual pilgrimage to Makkah, and the fifth pillar of Islam. A male who has performed *hajj* is called *hajji*, and a female *hajja*.

HIJRAH Migration. Refers to the migration of the Prophet Muhammad (pbuh) from Makkah to Madinah in 622 CE. Also means the leaving of all home ties for the sake of Allah.

IBADAH All acts of worship.

IFTAR Breaking of the fast each day during *Ramadan*.

IHRAM The state entered into when performing *hajj* or *umrah* (pilgrimage to Makkah at any time during the year). It also refers to the two pieces of white cloth worn by men and the normal modest clothing worn by women.

IHSAN Spirituality.

ITIKAF Special study of the Qur'an during *Ramadan*.

JIHAD Struggle for Allah.

KA'BAH The sacred shrine (a cuboid building) in the Grand Mosque in Makkah, said to have been built by Adam (pbuh) and rebuilt by Ibrahim (pbuh).

MUEZZIN The person who calls Muslims to prayer.

NABI (plural: *anbiya*) Prophet.

NIYYAH Right intention.

QIBLAH WALL The wall in a mosque, aligned with Makkah, that Muslims face when praying.

RAK'AH Fixed set of actions performed during *salah*.

RAMADAN The ninth month of the Muslim calendar; the month of fasting.

RASUL (plural: *rusul*) A messenger of Allah.

REVELATION A message received from Allah.

SALAH The five set, daily prayers. The second pillar of Islam.

SAWM Fasting from just before dawn to until sunset. The fourth pillar of Islam.

SHI'AH Members of a branch of Islam which separated from the orthodox Sunnis in 679 CE due to differences about the succession after the death of Muhammad (pbuh). They represent about 20 per cent of the Islamic world.

SUBHAH Prayer beads used to count recitations of the names of Allah.

SUFI Muslim mystic.

SUNNAH Model practice. The practice of the Prophet Muhammad (pbuh).

SUNNI Followers of the Sunnah of the Prophet Muhammad (pbuh). About 80 per cent of Muslims in the world are members of the Sunni tradition.

TAQWA Piety or consciousness of Allah.

TARIQAH The inward journey of the spirit.

UMMAH The worldwide Muslim community.

WUDU Ritual purification, ablutions performed before *salah*.

ZAKAH Giving money to the poor, especially at the end of *Ramadan*. The third pillar of Islam.

Index